Spring 2023

MUSE

Volume 37

Riverside City College

Riverside, CA

© 2023 MUSE Literary Journal

Published by students at Riverside City College
4800 Magnolia Avenue
Riverside, CA 92506

COVER ART:
front cover - Zeima Kassahun - Sunrise - alcohol ink
back cover - Alondra Montes Martinez- Rainy City Nights - acrylic

RCC MUSE is published annually and accepts submissions of fiction, nonfiction, and poetry.

ISBN-13: 978-0-9960411-9-5

PROSE | POETRY | ART

TABLE OF CONTENTS

INTRODUCTION

Leading up to the publication of this year's edition of *MUSE*, our team hosted an open-mic poetry reading at the Center for Social Justice & Civil Liberties in Downtown Riverside, hosted by the poet James Coats. The first reader signed up under the name Sincerely Heard. She boldly walked to the microphone without a notebook, no phone in hand. Her performance of a poem about a brother lost to police brutality had the room silent in emotional awe, as her voice resonated with power when describing the bright memories of him, and softened with pause and quiet retrospection as she came to terms with the loss of him and countless others. This set the stage for a night that represented the philosophy of *MUSE*, that through artistic expression of real emotions, we learn, we heal, and we advocate for our community. The final reader of the night recited a poem about being confronted in a grocery store while speaking Spanish by a woman who asked her, "Do you even speak English?" Her poem asked, "When you ask me if I speak English, do you really mean to ask me if I belong?" Before reading, the poet introduced her young son, who had recently been diagnosed with nonverbal autism. She explained that she brings him to as many poetry readings as she can so that he can hear and absorb the words, so that he can know that he has a voice too and that he can use it. This is what *MUSE* is about, and why we strive to publish the typically underrepresented from year to year. All of our voices have power, and from that collective power, change *can* happen.

Reader, as you hold this book in your hands, we invite you to consider each possibility just as we did. We chose each piece with the intention that it would make a difference for someone. We ask you that as you engulf yourself in each word and image, you imagine the long nights of each artist and writer as they brought these ideas to fruition. Whether that someone is a future editor, a struggling writer, a person isolated because of who they are, or someone looking for the right line in the right poem that will keep them going for just another day. As editors, we recognize the rare and amazing opportunity we have to bring this book to life. However, we are only granted that privilege through the awing vulnerability of other creators to trust us with their pieces. One of the most terrifying and yet most gratifying parts of creating is simply asking others, "Do you see me for who I am, and are you willing to accept it?"

If there is one thing we have embraced during the editing process of this edition of *MUSE*, it's the inherently chaotic nature of creativity. As much fun as it is to create this book, every editor that sets foot into our class has had to look at each submission, each individually crafted piece and ask themselves: what is the *point*? Being involved in the creation of this book has reminded us all not only of the influence we have as editors, but also as students, writers, artists, poets, and people that are simply looking for community, for change, and for connection with the vast world around us.

We're humans, social beings. Communication is a key component of our existence. Being able to express what we repress throughout our lives is therapeutic, whether it's bad or good baggage. Facilitating the creative outlets of others is what *MUSE* represents. The many glimpses of other people's lives through our literary art journal humbles and grounds us. It is an honor for us at *MUSE* to be the platform of the many vices creatives utilize on a daily basis to maintain our mental alacrity and conquer the obstacles that life has placed in front of us. We are all on our own independent journey, and at the end of the day, we are all humans playing with the cards we have been dealt.

We've experienced a multitude of different lives, moments, and characters throughout each word we have read this semester. Confinement, whether trapping our physical selves or constricting our minds. Love, disintegrating from childhood realities or sustaining through the most unlikely people. Identity, whether using it as a shield to protect ourselves and others, or grappling with the disquieting reality of who we truly are and who we should be. More than anything, this edition represents the complex nature of simply choosing to go on. Writing itself is the choice to add just one more word. *MUSE* would never be where it is today if it weren't for our previous editors, choosing everyday to support our cause. Years later, we are still sustaining because of the hope and vigor of students and writers we have never spoken a word to. We hope that years down the road, *MUSE* will still be sandwiched on your shelf, dog-eared, penciled in, highlighted, and hopefully loaned to many people you care about.

The material we have carefully selected to be in this year's edition touch on the human experience of joy and sorrow while also demonstrating the beauty of art that comes out of their stories. Their experiences touch a part within ourselves that captivate our hearts and minds, allowing us to rejoice in the triumphs and memorialize the defeats of our own experiences. We all come to a point in our lives when we question whether continuing our journey will lead us to new light or darker moments. We hope that these stories encourage you to embrace your light while keeping the valuable lessons you've learned while in the dark.

As we reflect on our time spent on this edition, we can't help but feel sad that our time together is coming to a close. Despite this, it will be our turn to pass the torch to next year's group of student editors. While selecting the pieces of prose and poetry to include in this edition, there became an emerging theme of the brevity of life. Although we are all sick of hearing about it, the pandemic taught us nothing if it didn't teach us to value the time we have, with ourselves and with others. Some of our pieces, as you'll see, inhabit the very being of reflecting on life and how it can very easily be wasted. From the trailblazing voices of new generations to the final print on the page, we only hope *MUSE* will inspire you all to keep writing this story alongside us.

It is with a bittersweetness that we'd like to give our thanks to everyone who supported us along our journey. First and foremost to our dynamic and steadfast professor, James Ducat, who has encouraged our independence, creative risks, and has fought tooth and nail for the opportunities and advancements that *MUSE* has been given. Furthermore, we'd like to thank our talented designer Gabriel Nava for his help with our amazing cover choice, our donors for their everlasting support, our submitters for their infinite creativity, and our readers for their continuing curiosity of what will come next from the editors at *MUSE*.

Jennifer Florez, Matthew Alfonso, Brett Bachman,
Alondra Montes Martinez, & Sierra Williams
RCC *MUSE* Editors

THE HOLDEN VAUGHN SPANGLER
MEMORIAL AWARD FOR POETRY

The Holden Vaughn Spangler Award
for the Best Poem about a Child or Childhood
was established in 2019 to honor the passing
of Dr. Jason and Stephanie Spangler's
eleven-year-old son.

Dr. Spangler is a member of RCC's English
and Media Studies Department.

*The judges have selected the poem
"The Quiets of Parenting," by M.A. Dubbs
as the winner of this year's award.*

Honorable mentions:

"When Shadows Walk," by Laura D. Weeks

"Past Dream Storms," by Madi Zins

Short list:

"A Different World," by James Coats

"What to Expect: The Teen-Age Years," by Cati Porter

The Quiets of Parenting
by M.A. Dubbs

I thought parenting would feel so big,
something loud and momentous,
like on the day you were born.
But I guess in a world of billions
there's nothing too special
about your creation or arrival.

Instead it's a collage of tiny things,
spiderwebs that weave and link
to display the connection
we have formed beyond sharing blood.
Something about the existence of you
Makes me love the mundane,
So I can yearn for the day-in, day-out.

In the chaos and redundancy of getting ready,
the reptition of food preparation
and snack dispension,
and wound healing,
and tuck-ins,
as endless as it all may seem,
I find peace in you.

Such big emotions in such a small frame
that I cradle, embracing you and myself,
in a security I could only imagine
when I had a frame much like your own.
 How can there be so much of me in you
when I love you so deeply?

It's a million quiet moments
when I have been so afraid
of silence.
So afraid that I couldn't do this
and never be enough for you
and all that you deserve
because you deserve nothing less
than absolutely everything.
It's the release to realize
that I have always been enough,
enough for the both of us.
How can you save my soul
by simply resting against me?
How do you fill my Earth with creation
in millions of voiceless ways?

Holden Vaughn Spangler Award Winner

When Shadows Walk
by Laura D. Weeks

Read only children's books.
Cherish only childish thoughts.
                    - Osip Mandel'stam

Children fold up so small at night.
Their unquiet limbs,
stilled in impossible poses,
shrink from your touch like sea anemones.
The largest of them
could fit into your palm.

Their things, so underfoot
by day, at night acquire
a sudden gravity.
Dolls, becalmed, stare
with transatlantic eyes-
foreign emissaries conspiring quietly
in nooks, on bookshelves.

Children are adepts,
bypassing the possible
for the implausible.
Children are obsessive:
their rules and rituals,
their whiter whites
and deeper cuts.

When shadows patrol the halls
grown-ups see corridors,
closet doors, cellars, storage,
steerage. Children see
wardrobes with fur trees,
attics, shipwrecks,
faces like fishes-
portholes for eyes.

Holden Vaughn Spangler Award Honorable Mention

Past Dream Storms
by Madi Zins

last night I visited a yellow treehouse
with a ladder to the attic where
Bill Clinton sat talking to himself.
not the same, they're not the—

they weren't, this dreamhouse and
the one of memory that had
sheltered me in my childhood
home's backyard that day it hailed.
(not rain, they're not the—)

and I, 5, exiled through sheets of
cubes of ice, far from the brick one
my parents stayed in.
I thought the plastic could cave in,

each ice cube pummeling
the familial mystique.
not the same, they're not the same to me.

I did not have my dolls have
sexual relations in that house,
but if I'd known how,
we'd all been blown.

Holden Vaughn Spangler Award Honorable Mention

A Different World
by James Coats

The most difficult part about this whole thing
is how do I get the kids to reconcile
staying ten toes down while not sinking six feet deep.
The streets call to our baby so young
turns them into little soldiers for blocks
that will never bleed or grieve for them.
They give their lives on these concrete beaches
of Normandie and Western, Crenshaw and Florence.
D-Day is every day when birth into tragedy

I don't have the kind of paper that buys influence.
The kind that can keep moms home from work.
The second job is need for a roof and bread
a bed and rest seldom exist for more than a moment.
They only learned rules in schools
never anything that made sense
their teachers only make cents.
They can make the teachers monthly pay in a weekend
plus school never took an interest in them
and let's not get started on all the missing men.
How are they supposed to learn masculinity
when pop's is part of the mass incarcerated
prison populated with their family and friends
a long life is only found in a life sentence.

What can I convince these children to live for
when they've already decided the neighborhood's
respect is the only thing worth dying for.
When they don't feel their life is even their own.
When they've never felt an ounce of love at home.
How can I know being more alone
than never wanted, every place I've been.

In extreme situations of survival who am I to judge
the jungle consumes all that is not dangerous.

Here sweet dreams are mythical creatures
when sleep in the jaws hell's contempt.
I could say we care about them
that they could choose another life
but we both know it would be a lie.
I would have to give them a different set of eyes.
They've already seen too much to smile
and believing in a different world.
might as well be their final fantasy.

What to Expect: The Teen-Age Years
Cati Porter

A distant echo, like fruit belched up from breakfast,
I remember how it felt to house your body in my body,
how it knobbed up to meet the palm of my hand,
how every gas bubble even before you could
was a kick. Then, you grew. Plop, you fell out of me
like a menarche clump of red cells except you
were pink and frail and required oxygen.
Then, suddenly, you were pushing up to standing,
walking, running, playing Matchbox cars,
and now here you are, only a toddler, with your own
car and license and my time is my own again
and I don't know what to do with it.
There was nothing to prepare me for this.
I read *The Baby Book* until the spine cracked
and pages leaked out like my nipples oozing milk
whenever you cried. I read *What to Expect When...*
each stage a fresh new hell, except, once you hit
puberty, there were no guidebooks to tell me
how to teach you to drive, how not to wind up in the ER
after a drinking binge, how to make you love
poetry, or me. That book doesn't exist, but I imagine
if it did it might begin with a chapter or two
on mourning what you'll never be.
Forget college. Forget the golf scholarships.
Never mind that homework. I forgive you for giving up
on my not giving up on you. I give you
the freedom to fail, and my unwavering love
as I watch you clamor at the guardrails,
pulling yourself back up, up, and then off again,
while I sit here barely daring to sip my glass of wine,
phone beside me, volume high, waiting, waiting.

Holden Vaughn Spangler Award Short List

Wild Violets
by Jennifer Phillips

Here's a simple truth of a careful garden:
some plants must find unequal welcome here.
One helper, hired to garden for my mother
at ninety, thought wild violets divine,
transplanting some from the woods among the herbs.
After a decade of eradication,
mats of them still appear each early spring,
clotting the shoots and roots of all their neighbors.
Miss a mere fragment, they will reproduce
a hundredfold. Pretty at first, like lies,
they change the landscape, spread and rule for the worse.
So small, they have power to distort the whole design
as the seemingly-innocent becomes malign.

Untitled *Briseyda Batz*

Blackout
by Zach Murphy

My roommate took off right before I lost my job at the pizza place. The only thing he left behind was a note that read, "Moved back home." If only the unpaid rent were attached to it.

I sit at the wobbly kitchen table, gazing at the floating dust particles that you can only see when the sunlight shines in at the perfect angle. Sometimes, you have to convince yourself that they aren't old skin.

The air conditioner moans, as if it's irritated that it has to work so hard. I haven't left the apartment in four days, for fear that the hellish temperature might melt away my spirit even more. *Is a heat wave a heat wave if it doesn't end?* I gulp down the remainder of my orange juice. The pulp sticks to the side of the glass. It always bothers me when that happens.

As I stand up to go put my head into the freezer, the air conditioner suddenly goes on a strike of silence and the refrigerator releases a final gasp. I walk across the room and flip the light switch. Nothing.

There's a knock at the door. I peer through the peephole. It's the lady with the beehive hair from across the hall. I crack the door open.

"Is your power out?" she asks.

"Yes," I answer.

"It must be the whole building," she says.

"Maybe the whole city," I say.

"The food in your fridge will go bad after four hours," she says. I'd take that information to heart if I had any food in the refrigerator.

"Thanks," I say as I close the door.

When the power goes out, it's amazing how all of your habits remind you that you're nothing without it. The TV isn't going to turn on and your phone isn't going to charge.

There's another knock at the door. It's the guy from downstairs who exclusively wears jorts.

"Do you want a new roommate?" he asks.

"What?"

He nods his head to the left. I glance down the hallway and see a scraggly, black cat with a patch of white fur on its chest.

"It was out lying in the sun," the guy says. "Looked a bit overheated, so I let it inside."

Before I can say anything, the cat walks through the doorway and rubs against my leg.

"Catch you later," the guy says.

I fill up a bowl with some cold water and set it on the floor. The cat dashes over and drinks furiously.

At least water is free, I think to myself. *Kind of.*

I head into my dingy bedroom and grab the coin jar off of my dresser. "This should be enough to get you some food," I say.

I step out the apartment door and look back at the cat.

"I think I'll call you Blackout."

In fear
by Joyce Meyers

Wisps of cloud drift on the lake's surface,
eyelashed in green reflections. The air
drips with peace, scent of almost-autumn.

I sense them before I see them, twisted
shapes rising from tall grass. Stilled
by my footsteps on the path, they stand

at attention. I still myself,
tumbling into wonder: four pairs
of antlers above eight gazing eyes.

I watch them watching me. They're wary,
though I, unweaponed, a fraction of their size
and strength, could easily be torn apart

by antlers engineered and honed for combat.
Yet it is they that fear while I
want only to hold this moment,

to gaze in silence, in reverence,
while the world about me
rolls toward apocalypse.

How to find the language
to let them know I mean no harm,
want nothing of them

but to drink their beauty,
reach out of my solitude
to love a living thing.

To reassure them, I avert my eyes,
walk on, hoping they will hear
my silent message. Yet they flee,

and tomorrow will again, the fear
of what is strange too deep
to yield to reality or reason.

Gone Fishing *Cherie Woods*

[kweer]
by Jordan Loveland

Sitting with a friend under the back porch of one of my childhood homes, we read through an old Merriam-Webster dictionary. We had a dearth of books within the house and the library was always closed whenever my parents returned from work—not that they would have taken us, not that the library was any good or allowed us to check anything out. Our young minds were bored and full of curiosity that could not be sated by our elaborate imaginations. We had gotten to the tail end of Q when I found a word that seemed to imprint itself onto my soul. With no usage notes, the entry gave only two similar definitions:

a.   differing in some way from what is usual or normal: ODD, STRANGE, WEIRD

b.   ECCENTRIC, UNCONVENTIONAL

I thought about how people had described me as odd or weird. How they said that I had an unusual way of doing things and an eccentric personality. Following the pronunciation guide, I let the sound roll over my tongue and out my mouth. I liked the way it felt; I said it again. My friend and I discussed how funny it was to say, how much it sounded like its synonym but cooler, and how we hadn't ever encountered the word before.

Young and bookish, I would often vow to use newly discovered words in my everyday speech. I rarely got the pronunciations right. My speech impediment was worse when I was younger, I struggled to decipher the phonetic alphabet system, and I did not hear a large variety of words spoken if they did not come from the television or radio (which I often could not hear with clarity, because I have always been partially deaf). My parents are of a limited lexicon. Most unknown things were called whatsits, thingamajigs, or thingamabobs accompanied by the descriptive implications of hands waving and gestures. But I like words and I get a certain sense of joy when I say one that is rarely used. Defenestrate (to throw out of a window) is a nice one, but difficult to work into a casual conversation.

Not much later I learned the danger of words. I was out in the field with my mother, we were investigating something—I'm not sure what, an anthill or a fallen tree limb—and I wanted to remark on how strange this natural phenomenon had been.

"Huh," I said, "how queer."

It ended badly. I was "never ever to say that word. Do you hear me? Never." With a dappling of bruises on my arm and a new item on the "Things Not to be Said Around Mother" list, I rushed inside and began to love my strange new word in secret.

With age came more understanding. This word was associated with heathen rainbows and The Gays; sins not to be loved and sinners to be saved; Ellen Degenerate and McLesbians; He-She-Its and Target. None approved, all to be avoided.

My friends and I, now pre-teens, played these funny little What-If games. If I was a boy, or you were a boy, would we date each other? What would be different about me, or you, if we were boys? We all conferred with each other, anxious over our budding sexualities and the noticing not just of boys, but of girls. Pretty girls. Afraid of eternal damnation, we all agreed: Girls were pretty, it's in their nature, and there's nothing unusual about admiring. With our purity rings and promise necklaces, we were good, upstanding heterosexuals. If you ignored what we did at any given sleepover or single-sex slumber party, playing Truth or Double Dog, Electric Chair Dare where one must remove an article of clothing for each lie or skipped action.

We gushed about Johnny Depp and fondled each other through a Captain Jack Sparrow print throw blanket. We hid our hair in ball caps, scribbled on mustaches in washable marker, and roleplayed the only type of dates and weddings we knew—that is, the heterosexual ones. We romanced each other and, when prompted, said that we were only very close friends.

In a more chaste social circle—a homeschooled one full of religious zealots and girls who showed only their hands and faces, who never wore make-up and only styled their hair in plain down or a low pony or braid, whose mothers called beautiful girls whores because their sons were being tempted away from Christ—I arrived at a park celebration hand-in-hand with my then best friend. It shocked the girls and, sequestered away from the rough and rowdy boys, they questioned us with keen interest.

"We're besties," we explained, "so we had a bestie-wedding and now we're wives."

My friend punctuated this by grasping my jaw and landing a loud kiss on my cheek.

One girl pressed, "Doesn't that make you," she hushed her tone, "gay?"

"Nope. We can hold hands, cuddle, and kiss like that because we're married."

A round of stunned gasps and revelatory looks rippled through the small crowd of girls.

They quickly split into pairs, excitedly holding hands and proclaiming, "We want to get married. We want to be each other's wives!"

So, on a sunny day under a maple tree at a public park, we held bestie-wedding after bestie-wedding in a fervor of friendship. We gifted our affection and felt no shame. The parents discovered our antics eventually, having whittled it out of some daughter or another, but we had been free and would never unknow the ecstasy of love without judgment.

Because I lost contact with these girls over a decade ago, I couldn't say with any confidence whether some of these girls might have developed fully as lesbians, bisexuals, asexuals, or gender-nonconformers. We expressed that day not a declaration of queerness, but a platonic adoration that had been restricted. I broached voting age as queer identifying. From my lips fell my favorite word, chanted like a prayer: "We're here, we're queer, get used to it."

When my father asked how he was supposed to explain it to people, I said, "Tell them I'm queer."

"But that word..." He trailed off, and I expected the hesitation because he was an 80s teen from Mormon Country, Idaho. "Isn't it bad?"

"It's not a slur, Dad." He gave me a look, the doubt clear on his face. I sighed. "Don't use it as a slur and it's not a slur. If people ask," I repeated, "tell them I'm queer."

Grandmother and Abuela
by Chris Goldsmith

Grandmother was born in New York City
and Abuela in Mexico City and they both raised

families near the border and they both had faithful
hard-working husbands and they both had sons

who served for this nation in faraway
battles and they had daughters

who attended colleges and my grandmothers
both eloped, rebelling against their families. And then

one wondered why her daughter
ran off and married and didn't tell anyone.

Both drank black coffee in the early afternoon
both had faith and they both voted

each election and both watched the local
news pretty much every day, and went grocery

shopping with lists, one believed in roast beef
and potatoes, and one in frijoles and tamales,

both drove cars and went for drives
with their husbands. A blanket and picnic meal in the

back seat and they both read, their
bookshelves beyond full. They enjoyed laughter.

One listened to the big band sound
the other Chavela Vargas. One had a piano.

They both died in strange rooms without
bookshelves and stereos. One television

tuned to soap operas and the other
novellas with the sound hardly on.

I Am a Nigerian Flower
by Oyeleye Mahmoodah

They say Nigerian flowers are weeds
That every page you flip of our story is made from inferior paper
But, I am nature, matured; I cannot fake what I am
My eye is soil, the black of clay and my skin is the anthill
My hair owns the woods, dense, deep and my head is
a canopy—the forest and its hierarchy
My teeth remind you of fangs and my lip is the beak
I am the crawling bird who swims, and I am amphibian
My body is a temple, hieroglyphics were scribbled
on its walls, but reborn in henna
These nail plates are an extension of the tree on my hands
And I have paws which leave prints
whether shielded or bare, I am an animal
and I accept the joy of being one
There is more to me than me, because
the essence of me is in me
I am royalty just like the purple hibiscus I am yet to plant
I don't hold sight in my eyes, but
I have it carefully tucked within my ribcage, sculpted
In my heart, on my palms,
I have seen not the garden, I need not to
For my body breeds nature
Nature is humane, luxurious, and free
I am the diary for nature lovers, for
I have found every one of its components
In what it means to be me
In the home, webbed within me.

Fly Free *Katherine Muñiz*

Dispatches From The Wilderness:

THE QUEER CASE OF YANNICK TRAVERS, FRONTIERSMAN

by M. Mort St. Marinos

OREGON COUNTRY, Feb. 29th, 1840 –
O Gentle Reader: It is I, your intrepid correspondent, Mort St. Marinos, humbly writing to you – as always – from far afield, astride my faithful mule (and closest confidant) Dapple. Today, I beg leave to recount for your edification the queer case of one Yannick Travers, Frontiersman, which began thusly: 'Ladies, gentlemen: This here "man" is a woman.'

The case was heard at the village green of Pauper's Saddle, a jerkwater of a settlement near Snake River. Alongside the accused, the principles in the trial were Judge Abner Adhelm, presiding; Reverend Nathaniel Brown, prosecuting; Horace Conner MD, witnessing — learned men all — and one Mrs. Colette (née Jardinier) Travers, a Parisian apothecary.

Formerly in the employ of the American Fur Co., Mr. Travers stood accused of 'crimes against Almighty morality,' when an anonymous parishioner discovered he was a she — Alas!, the lurid details of which you must intuit for yourself, Gentle Reader, as I dare not impugn your Christianly sensibilities — calling into question the legitimacy of Mr. and Mrs. Travers' union.

Following opening remarks, Dr. Conner upheld that beneath Mr. Travers' bearskin leathers he was 'naturally a member of the weaker sex.'

'There we have it,' Rev. Brown intoned, 'the very heart of the matter: This is not merely an act against Nature; it is an act against God, Himself!'

Speaking in his own defense, Mr. Travers rejoined in an ursine roar, 'I am, indeed, an act of God, sir: Beneath this bosom of Eve beats the heart of Adam.'

Lastly, the court heard from the bridegroom's bride: 'There is no better goodman on God's green earth than *mon* Yanni.'

Unmoved, Adhelm sentenced the erstwhile Mr. Travers to be publicly stripped of his hides and gowned in her silks; thus, annulled was their marriage.

Following sentencing, Travers took leave of Pauper's Saddle that next morning, electing for 'greener pastures further afield.' Readers can rest assured, Travers kicked up dust in a westerly course: Riding sidesaddle, bodice aflutter.

Later, at eventide, over chamomile tea — medicinally shared with yours truly — Ms. Jardinier admonished, 'The green here is too overgrazed to take root.' With jawline set, her gaze lingered on that setting sun.

Thus — as Tristan and Iseult damned to the Second Circle — the erstwhile Mr. and Mrs. Travers are but shadows borne onward. Of Travers, there has been nary hide nor hair since departure. Of Ms. Jardinier, upon your faithful correspondent's word, she, too, took her leave of Pauper's Saddle — aboard the eastbound stage.

As I saddled Dapple for parts unknown, Gentle Reader, we heard tell of one last queer coincidence I feel obligated to cheerlessly report: The most unfortunate passing of Rev. Brown, found dead, the victim of an apparent bear mauling.

Additional reporting by Théa-Marie Ryde

At the Library: Montréal, Quebec circa 1950
by Beth Brown Preston
for my father

Portrait of a Black man as scholar among ancient volumes:
Abandoned by his native country for Canada,
followed the North Star to the destination of his mind's
bright freedom.
His desire to write of the slaying of monsters:
"Then Beowulf spied, hanging on the wall,
a mighty sword, hammered by giants, strong and blessed
with a powerful magic, the finest of all weapons.
But so massive no ordinary man could heft
its carved and decorated length. He drew the sword
from its scabbard, broke the chain at its hilt.
Then savage with anger and desperate
lifted the sword high over his head
and struck Grendel dead with all the strength he had left...".

And the Black man wandered that library's dusty corridors
in a sacred building nestled on Montréal's steepest hills
gathering the endurance of mind to conquer his task:
to render the poem, so early it was sung only to kings,
a ballad, written by no one knows, yet passed on, in tradition,
glorifying the fierce and brave deeds of a warrior.

And the Black man himself became a warrior,
wielding the sword of language, fighting the good fight,
who basked in the light of a certain fame,
never worried about the consequences of his bravery,
save his own honor, of greater value than any poem.

The Black man rendered dreams a world without monsters.

Strawbunny *Jocelyn Mulgado*

gender mirror
by Mikey Bachman

not as she is, but as she fills his dream
—Christina Rossetti

her face is a renaissance painting
separate from (his) body, soft-toned,
belongs to the woman (that i am)
who seals it away from this world,

who beats her belly with her fists
(*his* fists) in the hope of breaking it,
who tears from herself the outline
of an hourglass from (his) broadness,

who drives her hand into the mirror
and plucks (his) body of dead flower,
rips its belly-fat with clawed fingers,
replaces it with smooth, skinny love,

who scans herself as a grocery-worker,
tags (his) body with the price of *error,
please restock,* who won't look at (him)
and even dare mouth the word *love,*

who offers each day to take the place
of (his) body in the mirror just to see
herself as she wants to be, as she is,
who paints her body as she dreams.

Quinceañera
by Alexandra Geiger Morgan

She stands there blooming on our late afternoon walk from El Llano Park, on the terrace of San Matias Jalatlaco Church in Oaxaca. Her cascading pink dress flares around her feet like the bell in the tower that rings for her.

There she is, beautiful to behold, flanked by the generations of women in her life, being presented to her world. A 15-year-old bud, prepared to be plucked. As she stands there looking petulant and annoyed, the entire crowd passing by on the street witnesses her glorification. Castilian men, musicians in dramatic gold and black brocade costumes play as younger men dance, spin, leap, and somersault before her.

She stands, wooden and unsmiling, tolerating this ritual, as a giant flower might be resentful of its own beauty about to bloom.

Now the dancers and band have finished. The virgin has been whisked away quickly in a long white limo as the bell tolls 15 times and the plaza continues to empty.

How I long for that kind of reception for my own coming of age. As I stand there on the empty plaza, I recall the scene of my own debutant rite of passage. It does not take place on the plaza of our parish church, St. Andrew's, in Pasadena, California, but in my bedroom at home.

I am 15 years old, and I am awakened by my father forcing me down on the bed in my room. As my father holds my arms, my mother beats me with a leather belt. No words are spoken. I know what this is about. My mother continues with her full force until I am unconscious. I regain consciousness on the floor next to my bed to the sound of the doorbell ringing. My parents are gone and therefore do not answer it.

I open the door to a girl in a pastel yellow uniform from my carpool, Lisa Sloman. I see her father parked out front in the vintage black Mercedes, engine running. I tell her that I'm not feeling well and can't come to school today.

From the look on her face, I can tell she knows it's more than that.

From then on, I am no longer completely in my body. I ride my bike to and from school every day and everywhere else I need to go. I do not realize that the powerful need that prohibits me from getting in their car again, where they can see me up close, is shame.

The incident is not mentioned by me or my parents ever again.

My coming of age will not be a celebration.

Amelia *Leah Felty*

And for a second
by Ivana Gonzalez

And for a second
I felt what Icarus must've felt
When he soared over the sea

The wind in my hair
The sun in my face
Watching the clouds roll by in the bright, blue sky
Feeling like a feather fighting against gravity

Then it all came to a crash
As my little nine year old body hit the pillows and blankets we had
Stuffed inside the rickety, old trampoline
That I quickly climbed out of to run back inside

Up the stairs and into the biggest bedroom
With the screenless window wide open
Watching and waiting as the other girls also threw themselves out
Onto the trampoline

The room was filled with giggles as each of us waited for our turn
One by one
One child after another
Like little lemmings jumping off cliffs

Out the window we go
Each of us trying to recreate
That new sensation

We were all Icarus that day
Peter Pan and Tinkerbell
Angels

Stupid little girls
Without pixie dust or wings
                        Learning to *fly*
                            To *fall*
                    To *do it all again*

With a smile on our faces the whole time

Water bear x potted nopal *Jeni*

My Neurons are Plotting Against Me
by Claire Scott

I can hear them rustling and whispering
at night when my mind spins
like a vinyl record on a turntable
planning a mutiny like the H.M.S. Bounty
tired of the load they've been carrying
for almost eighty years
tired of no breaks, no birthday cakes
no swanky watches every ten years

One large group leaving for Miami
to lie on bikinied beaches
and get blotto on margaritas, no possibility
any words starting with s or l
or the names of my ten cousins

Another taking a train to Las Vegas
to gamble at MGM Grand and ogle strippers
goodbye to words with capital letters
as well as the names of green vegetables

The smallest group, less spunky, will go
to a local movie or maybe a Giants game
but even so, for a few hours I won't remember
any words with two syllables
or words that rhyme with *now*

I can see my restless neurons need a raise
from my ever-dwindling resources
(rent not paid, Top Ramen again)
before they form a union
and demand all-expense-paid sabbaticals
to Marrakesh or Madrid, leaving me struggling
to find the name of my dog
and my password to Amazon

Untitled *Leah Felty*

Little Box
by Kendal McGinnis

You spend your time after the funeral picking up
your life and saying goodbye to it. You do the kinds of jobs
that men who give you unsolicited advice say will make you
interesting later. So you're in Concord, Massachusetts wearing
an orange vest and a walkie and non-slip shoes with steel
toes going around saying Mel do you copy and Mel says yes
I copy. People have big ideas now. Mel included. Tik Tok
speaks to Neoliberalism so she has the term and can give a
small Ted Talk on American puritanical values and how
we're all imperialists who fashion ourselves the underdog
but no one's going to mention you or how you're in non-slip
shoes and an orange vest walking around going Mel do you
copy. Mel's an encyclopedia on juice. She can tell you about
the dawn of the company's foundation, where the grapes come
from, its exhibition at the Chicago World Fair in 1893. But
she's embarrassed by Concord. The city layout is as mundane
as any other New England town, a McDonald's, a Starbucks, a
stoplight with hanging telephone wires, a spider-webbed Best
Western along the expressway. But Concord is a family of lazy
settlers. Twenty minutes by car from Plymouth Rock. No one's
ancestors or posterity here ever manifest destiny-ing. It's just
the spot to live and die.

Anybody, says Mel, can go on Google and search
what it is to be a working-class American. Mel says this in
big hoorahs through several layers of personal protection
equipment. But no one will mention what it feels like to bend
over and fixture a gasket between a pipe and valve and pump
juice from the tank in cellar nine to the tank in the backlot.
That is for sure. Just wait thirty-six years. The vest and the
walkie'll become you. The big black shoes, the Levis, you'd
never guess we're not all dykes here laughs Mel, a hearty jostling
sort of laugh. Oh boohoo, don't fret, it's not homophobia, it's
just that defense mechanism that saves from waning and aging
femininity, something to do with the working-class thing,
we'll circle back. You'll hear a variation of this joke another
hundred times anyway by the end of the harvest. Let's be clear,
you're making the nonalcoholic alternative to wine. A drink for
churchgoers, people with good American values.

Taking to heart unsolicited advice from men becomes
a quirky part of your personality. You'll see later. These men
are more or less a demographic. They think you're funny
when other people think you are too quiet or too crude. You

remind them — but of course not too much — of their own daughters. They save you. They take you under their wing. You have a landlord in Leadville, Colorado, where you do another one of the jobs that are beside the point, that takes you out one night and buys you bratwursts at a brewery on the town's main street which is called Main Street. Jim is his name. Three or four beers you drink together.

Jim is handsome in the groomed, cheery, recent-Colorado-property-owner kind of way. A face that says: a positive spin! — an upward spiral! His move from the West Coast has something to do with taxes and also maybe a new hunting law or a wolf sanctuary nearby — you miss that part between sips of beer and the brewery is loud and buzzing with people. No clink of ski boots or gloves being tossed on the table, none of that. It's sort of a dreamy local crowd on this night. Men that plow the runs, college boys who check your tickets, a neighborhood restaurant owner and his wife. Jim's monologuing — it's characteristic of the demographic. You've heard at this point about his divorce from Trudy, the whole thing was sort of slow-burn or that's how you read it, probably he tells you too about his daughter in Humboldt County failing out of a Communications major. You notice things are weighing on him and you grab his hand. There's an intimacy between you and Jim. Something you've had before and will again with men that give advice so laudable it transcends whole generational boundaries, job markets, gender divides.

You start sleeping one day with one of these men. Craig or something. He lives in a swanky but minimalist apartment overlooking the Pulaski Bridge (on the Brooklyn side, obviously). He's much older than you but jogs and stays away from red meat. His mattress and books are on the floor. The view is spectacular and the books on his floor are all ones that quirky Bushwick girls your age love: the Zadie Smiths, the Aimee Benders, the Lidia Yuknavitches. Craig is a little shamefaced about his studio. He used to work in homeland security, but his conscience gets the better of him. Now he's at a hedge fund in the city. We're all a little implicit, he whispers to you as you lean with your back against the kitchen sink, his hands gripping the counter on either side of you, maybe his thumb in one of your belt loops (in a hot way not a predatory way). In 2001 he was working in the Pentagon, he says. You try to mimic the expected jaw-drop he's after. Craig was there on the day it all happens. He doesn't ask you of course about your own 9-11 story because you would've been too young to have a personal anecdote. Mostly likely he doesn't care anyway. There's no time for that now. The fact alone that he was in the Pentagon on the day it all goes down, he's using your generation's lingo now, getting really close to your ear, it makes women want to put out for him he says. He says it coyly, sheepishly, he's using "put out" sarcastically — it's ironic, no Greenpoint hipster would use "put out" and mean it. But don't worry, he's not really a hipster, he tells you this before you get to the part where you're between his hands leaning with your back against the kitchen sink. Craig's really self-aware. He shrugs his own narrative to the side in a lionhearted act of humility. You wonder later whether you sleep with him because you too are taken by the sheer valor of his Pentagon story or whether there's a look-at-me-now moment when you're undressing in front of the floor-to-ceiling window overlooking the Pulaski Bridge, the New York skyline big and bright before you, you can almost see the Chrysler Building, the Empire State, the TJ's on 3rd Avenue where the organic people go to get their Trader O's, all of it.

Jim's hand is getting soggy in yours. This moment means so much to him. Big, hunky conservative men are all softies, overly sentimental. They want the troops to come home or they want the troops to stay there or they want the troops to finish their duty but what the duty is is not the duty of these big, hunky conservative men to say, no. The American flag outside his Leadville log-cabin dream home says enough, doesn't it. Jim is a good listener. It makes him feel good that you take advice from him. He's crying now, babbling a bit, he's saying something like Trudy or troops or Truist — that might be his bank — who knows. You can't tell, he's too wet and too pink. Men with fresh snow still in their beards begin looking over at you at your table, which is elevated. The seats themselves are old whiskey barrels. The bar is original, from the original German pub, but everything else has that manicured renovation feel. A high yellow-lit ceiling with wooden beams running across it. Young healthy servers from Liberal Arts backgrounds, scruffy and intellectually worn-out but from well-off families. No one's been here before, but we've all been here before. It's just someone's take on an impression of something else. The more you move the more you understand this. Every town or city has a one-dimensionality to it. When you pick up your stuff and load the car and say good-bye, the town itself folds itself flat like the turned pages of a pop-up children's book until it's just a road and then a highway — the I-5 then the I-70 then the Indiana Expressway, all in your rear window. Home is not a place, home is the men who give you unsolicited advice.

A bearded man at the table parallel to yours mouths to you: Is he okay? Jim's mom — you've gotten to the bottom of it — is married and remarried seven times before Jim turns twenty-five. Add Trudy and the loser daughter into the mix and you have a recipe for a big, hunky man to break down at the gentle touch of your hand, the snow falling in silent sheets on the sidewalk outside, the old rickety bar and a sexy modern backsplash behind him. Jim leans in, squeezes your hand tighter. The chatter dies off. The brewery blurs away. It's just his puffy pink face. You almost know it's coming and then it comes. He grabs your cheeks dramatically, spontaneously, and pulls you close. He turns your head slightly and whispers into your ear, I have a little box. Jim has a little box and it is filled to the brim with bad and negative emotions. He just puts it, he says, on the edge of a small shelf high in his office and doesn't touch it except on dark days. Put it all in the box, divorce yes daughters yes death of an old touch-football friend him too his mother's marriages yesyesyes. Put it in the box. His box is metaphorical or at least that's what you're thinking. He looks at you so piercingly you worry he's going to dive into a kiss on your lips. Where is your box, he whispers. Huh. Where do you keep your little box?

Mel invites you to dinner at her house after your shift. It's fall and the harvest at the company is ending soon. Mel lives in West Concord, by the golf course. She looks nice, she has tomorrow off. Her dress is something floral, something silky. Oh this? She'll say. Target. Mel and her ex-husband lose everything in one way or another. A second mortgage taken out on a business gone underwater. Not to the Great Recession but to a corrupt business partner who flees to Florida says Mel's new man Pat. Not tonight Mel says, giving him a look. But Pat won't give it up, it's part of his own narrative now. You can't get to know him or eat dinner at their house in West Concord without hearing the whole shebang. Mel and her ex go bankrupt shortly after the evil business partner—the story's growing in melodrama, you like it. Mel divorces him as a last blow to the man's self-esteem and he dies shortly after. She meets her new man at the funeral, do you believe it? A romance out of dust and ash says Pat.

Mel serves watermelon. It's a cool orange-skied fall evening. Everything this mundane takes on meaning at a certain hour and the hour is now. The clouds seem to be going in all directions. Pat gives you one of his good beers from the refrigerator in the garage. He winks at you, like he's sharing a secret only you can be let in on. You're comfortable here in Concord, sitting on a porch with chipped paint and strung-up patio lights, the smell of something hot and baked in a dish smothered with cheddar. It smells so heavenly. Mel and Pat are laughing at each other. The conversation loses you but they're talking about money in a sort of playful way, writing off the hardship and anxiety with self-deprecation. You don't like when working-class people like you and Mel and Pat complain about cycles of poverty. It's much prettier when fluffy academics do it or you can read it in a book or something. But Mel and Pat don't matter much, they're just characters in one of your stories anyway, not real people like your dad. The dish is eaten and you are tired and Mel is scrolling Tik Tok in the dark. There are dogs barking coming from the screen.

Your little box is in the passenger seat and you are driving. It's a boring twenty minutes from Concord to Plymouth Rock. You've settled on reverse manifest destiny. The little box and you and the long trek across the country. You park your car in the visitor center parking lot. You're expecting it to be inconsequential and graffitied in something unintelligible but it's beautiful actually. Simple and complicated and holding so much history in its body. The beach before it is gated off because it's sacred to you and your ancestors and your posterity, the ones who make it out west. You hop the gate clutching your little box tight against your chest and walk it out past the shoreline.

Craig isn't all that bad you promise. The hugs he gives you after you buzz into his loft are big and breathy, all-encompassing. He hugs you like someone who loves your body, not for the body itself. Your dad used to hug you like that. Your dad wasn't perfect: A California transplant from Concord, Massachusetts. Came across as a reader but was totally not a reader. Made his way across America, stopping, working odd-jobs, becoming interesting. He did that thing that dads do where they compete to make their lives sound super adventurous but use self-deprecating language to do it so it shows humility and he was bashfully patriarchal but also a leftist so therefore complex and he was insistent about his Mayflower story, his 9-11 story, his retirement dream home in Colorado, everything subject to embellishment but never for malice. He's the guy that poemed and syntaxed you into existence. You miss the way he hugged. He lives in a little box now on your desk in-between the mascara and the two deodorants you can't decide on.

Mom Song
by J. Tarwood

1979

Candy dishes like watering holes.
Trek time.

Mom's lips suck away
on her Harlequin peppermints.

In the TV like nuzzling guppies,
Luke promises Laura

he'll never ever rape her again.
(On cue, Herb Albert trumpets *Rise*.)

Sugar's sizzled Mom's blood enough.
Now a big puff on that Camel cigarette.

Ready?
She looks out the window.

In the winter wind,
two laughing

High school girls, swinging
hair that's infinite moss.

They must reek like wolves.
Mom yearns

to shave them bald and pour their brains
like yolk on a hot skillet.

But look: Luke and Laura are eating at last.
They have such lovely teeth.

The steak squirts blood.
With gravy, mashed potatoes

are volcanoes melting right on through
the ice caps of their dinner plates

Fleeting Clew *Jacob Bowling*

Tweet
by Imari Rede

I saw the best minds of my generation destroyed by media,
Starving hysterical performance
Dragging themselves through the depths of despair
Looking for a smidge of validation,
Airheaded bimbos burning for deep connection,
Understanding what is thought to be out of reach,
Who are broke and beautiful and lay awake
Smoking weed to keep the demons at bay
Scrolling through Zillow contemplating grad-school
Who bared their brains to salvation under capitalism
Rihanna and Gaga angles staggering online opportunities
Bright like a diamond
Who passed through universities with designer undereye bags
Imposter syndrome California and debt- like tragedy among the
Scholars and whores,
Who expel themselves from academia, looking crazy & destroying
Generational odes through stained glass windows
Who cannot afford to no longer be their true selves
Money in virtual shopping carts and reading about black death on
every time line
Who bust their asses to make ends meet
Never without an eighth at hand
Who drink bottomless mimosas at brunch then make $100 last a week
Hallway, cry, or purgatoried body dysmorphia night after night
Endless streams of tits and ass
Incomparable images on the gram that insight value of the self
Front camera flip looking like the close up of Squidward with the pores and
shit,
Who forced themselves to make it through the week yet again
And came out to their POC family who hoped it was just a phase
Being a queer femme punk icon picnicking in a 3rd grade teacher thrifted
maxi dress
Who talked continuously 3 days straight, fell in love on twitter and met up
Found to be the one who was catfishing
Mean Girls word vomit to the group chat

So you agree?
Memories and personal tragedies told through memes, laughing at
Heartbreak, 51/50 and racism
Whole intellects deduced to an image with a message to be taken
One way or another, glamourized darkness or disdain for delight and true bliss
Who share a picture of a margarita and plate of shrimp tacos and like that more
than the accomplishments of their perceived loved ones
One small post to mark this second of pleasure to be grounded
In life as it flows through the air in a million little pieces and is projected onto
A screen held in hand cause there ain't no pockets in these pants

Relax Your Mind *Artistic Punk*

Apple Tree in a War Zone
by Claudine Griggs

The tree bore the full-blossomed apples of September though some of the branches suffered injuries from bullets or shrapnel. Otherwise, the great arbor stood firm and proud in what seemed a miraculous hundred-square-foot sanctuary surrounded by the scars of war. A mortar shell had landed over there; an unexploded grenade lay close by; a body fumed inside a burned tank across the field. Yet the apples grew ripe and luscious on low-hanging boughs that invited man and beast to a natural banquet. Trees don't discriminate. They dispense their life-giving fruit to the first-come, first-served.

Snipers knew this. And the woman perched upon the hill valued herself as one of the best riflemen in the country. She expected that sooner or later the enemy, who'd probably survived on C-rations for weeks or months, would value fruit more than the risk that might warn them away. They would want an apple. Their bodies would crave it. Nature's bounty among the vestiges of war.

And what a war this had been. First, there were guerilla skirmishes and political maneuvering. Then negotiations fractured and the "real" fighting began, which really meant that casualties were reported on the evening news instead buried in unit commanders' reports. The apple tree didn't understand or care about human affairs. It was perfectly designed to grow tasty pods for vertebrates that might scatter its seeds to new lands for reproduction. A sensible and natural purpose. Bombs and guns and killing were unknowns to vegetable matter, but not so to military humans or one of their snipers who continued to wait patiently on a rocky ledge for the enemy to arrive, relish the low hanging fruit, and reach for it. Then, that enemy would die from a precisely placed single bullet. And this lone shooter was good, very good. She rarely missed.

Still, the enemy was no fool and understood the rules of engagement just as well as the hidden sniper. Two sides of a double-headed coin. Either to kill or be killed, depending on their orders or luck or destiny, and neither would stroll casually into enemy sights. All life struggled to avoid death.

The hidden sniper waited for eight days, surviving on prepackaged food that tasted too much like straw, urinating and defecating in a shallow pit twelve feet beyond her deadly perch, waiting for a clear shot at any soldier reckless enough to succumb to a desire for succulent fruit. Of course, she and her commander hoped to take down a high-ranking officer, but there were few guarantees in war.

~+~

The sniper's name was Madeira. She was twenty-nine years old and had joined the Army when she graduated from high school. After basic training and tech school, Madeira decided that desk work was not her cup of tea. She hated tea partly because it reminded her of the British occupation of her country long before she was born, but the resentment of her forefathers had trickled down to her and taken a firm root. To her, this fragrant afternoon drink, sweetened or unsweetened, spiced or unspiced, hinted at colonial oppression.

Of course, the British and Americans had little to do with this war, just as the British and Americans wanted little to do with a sub-Saharan country that couldn't provide a noticeable benefit to their economies or national security. Madeira resented that, too. The Chinese and Iranians had offered military aid, but they had self-serving agendas that did not coincide with Madeira's vision of a free and independent homeland. A generous helping hand often came with a substantial debt in the balance. Very heavy. In fact, she suspected that Iranian officials were secretly aiding the enemy of her democratic government. Well, almost democratic. Yet Madeira believed in a forthcoming regime by the people and for the people. That's why she fought.

After the Army's recruit training, Madeira tried her hand with an M-16 on the base firing range. Even the most paternalistic officer could tell she was good with a rifle, and desperation for qualified and patriotic snipers outweighed their prejudice. After all, if the civil authority fell to the rebels, those same officers would be among the first to be rounded up, paraded before a new government, and publicly executed. Better to acknowledge a woman's skill than lose a war, and the enemy was more dangerous than women's rights.

At first, Madeira cared little beyond service to her country and developing skill as a sniper. But soon, she embraced a healthy competition with herself and others. Her longest documented kill-shot registered 975 yards. Sure, many American snipers had scored farther during the Afghan war, but they had superior rifles and scopes; and they had spotters to assist them. Madeira sniped alone, using only her talent, intelligence, and feminine patience. Those counted in this kind of fighting. They had also kept her alive for seventeen months in a drawn out civil war. And she understood that a woman killed in a little conflict was just as dead as a woman killed in a big one. She remained cautious. She meant to survive this bloodshed.

~+~

After Madeira had held her position at the sniper's nest for fifteen days, she began to wonder whether the enemy might be in retreat. No targets had approached the tree, which still hung low with ripening apples, although a few had fallen to the ground. "What a marvel," she thought, "for such life-giving boughs to survive the ravages of war with its surrounding earth bombed and scorched to hell and back." It would have seemed a miracle from scripture if she believed in gods. But this was wondrous, nonetheless, and Madeira did believe in many things. She believed that democracy would prevail and that she would one day rejoin civilian life, find a suitable husband, and create a loving family in a more secure world for everyone. And this would be no miracle. It would be a secular reward for people who held firm, did their duty, and rebuffed tyranny.

During her nested vigilance, Madeira had eaten nothing but C-rations, alternating canned meals of turkey loaf, tuna, ham and eggs, sliced pork, beans and franks, beef steak, chicken, and spaghetti with meat. A day's food package offered adequate protein, fiber, and vitamins but little flavor. It was hard to tell the turkey loaf from beef. Extra salt made the spaghetti palatable.

As a result, and because she had seen no enemy soldiers, Madeira started to pine for the fruit a mere 400 yards away from her camouflaged perch. A few crisp apples to supplement canned ham and eggs seemed deliriously appetizing after fifteen days. Then, perhaps, she'd hike back to her company station, report on the enemy's lack of movement, receive tactical updates, and ask for a new assignment. With any luck, the war might be winding toward its inevitable close. No one fights forever.

~+~

It was early next morning when, with still no enemy movement, Madeira emerged from her hidden nest, shouldered her scoped rifle, and began a walk toward the miracle tree. Maybe she'd even skip her C-rations today and just feast on apples. She could almost sense the juice running down her chin and the natural sugars invigorating her spirit before she returned to headquarters. This area was dead, so she might as well accept it and request new duties.

About 100 yards from the tree, Madeira noticed a bunny scamper into a mortar crater where it had dug into the loosened earth for added protection. Life amid war? It seemed that nothing could stop the humblest of creatures from overcoming the odds against them.

Finally, as Madeira approached the apple tree and marveled at its surging vitality, a tiny hummingbird, drenched with fluorescent color, alighted on one of the mid-range limbs, gazed at her without apparent fear, and then buzzed gracefully toward a higher branch where it groomed itself as though the remnants of war were irrelevant. Madeira felt a sense of joy that probably should not be felt here, and as she reached for a correspondingly beautiful piece of low-hanging fruit, there was a spray of vermillion liquid across the nearest branch. Madeira felt no pain but realized a sniper's bullet had pierced her neck.

"This one's a shooter," she thought.

Two seconds later, because snipers generally use bolt-action rifles, a second bullet splattered Madeira's chest on the way to her heart. She smiled in peculiar admiration of the enemy, and the last thing she remembered was a wondrous flash of iridescent color streaking from the apple tree to quieter ground.

Luke 12:32 *Dale Dewey*

Brother Snow
by Brian Daldorph

My brother was not a strong man.
He was always the last to be picked for a team
but he was strong in another way:
if he believed in something he'd do it,
nothing would stop him.

He left for basic training the day after his eighteenth birthday:
he was not going to be a supply clerk—
there was a war on so he was going to be a soldier.

The last time I saw him was the night before
he shipped out: we met for lunch, he ate well.
"I won't be coming home from this, you know.
Can you handle that, Jo? Can you help our mother?"
I said it was the least I could do.

He was dead in three weeks, bombed by his own planes.
Late September and, strangely, snow.
The snow that was beautiful, out of season,
and didn't last long.

Big Foot in Death at Wounded Knee *Victor Valencia*

Ballad of a Dishwasher
by J. B. Rossi

I've seen you here before. I've seen you in the same aisle as me. They ask us: How many drinks a week? We respond: How many beads are there in a rosary? And we ask ourselves the same question: What has the bottle given us?

I will tell you.

We have known the bedside manner of a woman from Tennessee. We have read the poetry of boomslangs, heard the paperback moods of a violin. We have conversed with the gharial in his Sunday best while the river drinks with us all day, and the Sun herself answers our prayers.

What has the bottle given us?

The other night, when it was 99 degrees at 8 p.m., and the air was still and heavy, I drank 100 proof from a plastic handle and, for the first time in my life, listened to Fats Domino. I was alone. I felt the heartbeat of a rainforest in my bloodstream.

That next morning, I wiped bile from the corners of my mouth and kicked dirt over the vomit that escaped before I made it to the curb. I was behind the steakhouse, and it was a few minutes before my shift. I lay crumpled by the curb, waiting on the good Lord to take me, waiting for my brain to explode.

I discovered a praying mantid a few paces from my eyes, frozen in space. Its front legs held up together, I saw a prizefighter of the animal kingdom, a featherweight, rather than one asking a higher power for help. The mantids struggle but absorb the blows we inflict upon them: habitat loss, pollution, an aggressively changing climate. We throw haymakers, but they stay in the ring.

I gathered some fast food wrappers on the pavement in front of me, clutching them like the hand of an old friend. I got up and washed dishes for twelve hours. No lunch. No breaks. I had the strength and the peace of mind. By the time my shift finally ended, I realized the praying mantid is the patron saint of dishwashers.

That night I reached for the bottom shelf, for deep time. I hurdled through ecstasy and annihilation in the company of hemlocks, owls and sports talk radio.

I studied the towering voice of Linda Rondstadt. Put Fats in again. Gave Meat Loaf a listen and danced wildly by the CD player.

When my blood alcohol climbed high enough, I wept and marveled at the Assumption of the Blessed Mother. And I felt, for a brief moment, that I was on the right side of life, that I was in the corner of the mantid with a towel and a bucket, that I finally belonged on this Earth.

The next morning, I wiped bile from the corners of my mouth and kicked dirt over the vomit that escaped before I could make it to the curb.

It would be a good day.

Craftsman at Riverside Lunar Festival *Joseph A. Perez*

Spain Comes to Visit
by Wendy L. Silva

But there are actually two Mexican games of chance,
one indigenous and ancient—patolli—and the
other European and Colonial—la lotería—that
apprise these contemporary pictures and words.
                                                    - Rupert Garcia

El gallo warned the neighborhood
in high-pitched prayer the morning she arrived.
I hadn't seen esa vieja in 192 years

though rumors had spread about even the stars
in her eyes imploding to be free
of her vision. All that's left are black stones

cratered in sapphire. I never know
if I'm looking at mar o cielo. Either way it's abundant,
this blue. Her first night back

we went for drinks. Bought her the cheapest
tequila, bragged about mis hijos
mestizos so she'd think I'd forgiven. If she only knew

I'd shredded her bandera like a legal document,
stuffed it in a cantarito to burn. Left the water
tasting of sweet clay and ash. Left my breath smoky.

Placing frijoles on the table, 50 pesos
to bid, she asked for the cards. Sifted
through hundreds to find hers: death in the top

row, el mundo resting at the bottom
with the weight of chance. I called the rhymes
until all I needed was el pájaro

with its gold-breasted feathers rising
from my hand. Instead, her hand
como un alacrán on my shoulder

saying *I'd never take tus centavitos,*
mija, as if a good step mother, the kind that leave
the house smelling of pork meat and spice. But she broke

my house. Brought fire from between sea
and sky and drove it through our flesh:
a forced implosion. Rebuilt our walls with smoke

and the color of mud drained from our faces. Tlaxcala,
Tenochtitlán, Teotihuacán—birds
fallen from our tongues. The years it took

to relearn flight after she'd put a rifle in my hand,
pointed its barrel at my head and said *this
is how you win the game.*

A Poem I Made Up of Random Texts From My Phone ft. My Friends & Me
by Ivana Gonzalez

Turn my trauma and tragedy into art.
I'm the main character but I'm in the wrong novel.
Too many plot twists makes a story tangled.
It's a good book, you should read it one day!
It's a marvelous death that occurs after finishing a book.

~+~

"*Chaos reigns supreme and I am merely a conduit.*
And yet I wish for the one thing I have;
My bounty is as boundless as the sea,
My love as deep;
The more I give to thee,
The more I have, for both are infinite"
As you can tell, I fuck with Shakespeare.
He's alone in an empty theater. What's left to perform?
You're pretty good at writing!
You only want me for my words.
I love you for you.
My intellectual prowess intimidates you so.

~+~

What did your Mom say?
The gods want you to continue talking to me.
Lmao my mom just told me God said gays go to hell again.
Go pray to your false gods.
There are good reasons to go to hell, that is not one of them.

~+~

How's that trauma coming along?
I keep throwing myself at a brick wall over and over again
Hoping it would fall first; spoiler alert, it didn't.
I hate him.
I hope he lives a long prosperous life without me,
And see all the places where I could've fit (but he fucked up).
He never deserved you

~+~

Dumb dumb dumb.
Meanie. Mean meanie. :(

You're beautiful.
How was your day?
It's okay, I'll be okay.
I love you. I love you. I love you.
I love you too.

~+~

Goodnight. I love you. Remember to look at the moon today.

Teapot *Zeima Kassahun*

What's the Smell of my mom's Cooking?
by Shannon Ward

Sprawled in the backseat of my mom's car,
all my senses awaken from a smell of delicious memories.

The flashing red and yellow neon sign--hurting my eyes
My nostrils are inhaling this old familiar land for a sense, a
reaching feel or more.

What is that smell, you ask?

It is undoubtedly a smell of a soul--pungent, flowing in the air
we breathe like a breeze against the world.

Grease entangles this small mind and body of five years.
Looking over the large seat, my mom is speaking to someone
I can't see
Outside was blinding, the grease was working its way from a
memorable smell to gut wrenching hunger.
There was no fear of something new or gross, just the same
thing…

Even though our apartment wasn't far,
despite my age making me seem smaller,
what I knew was that my fond memory was fast food everyday.

The tasty grease stain on my Ariel Little Mermaid nightshirt,
Every empty ranch cup hidden under the seats--
from nuggets and bitten fingers,
I can take every bite and tummy wouldn't hurt,
in the middle of the night, or these small fries on my hands.

"Want McDonald's?"
Nod!

"Want Taco Bell tonight?"

Nod, nod!

"What do you want from Jack in the Box's?"
Like a dashboard doll, my answer and head would always
nod.

Have you ever gotten sick of it?
Or are you just afraid to admit?

In a way, I am... Once--

Whenever my classmates had lunchtime,
all they had was these colorful boxes with strange things in
them...
Sweet red apple slices
Yellowy cheese bites
Small, small sandwiches
Tiny green juice boxes
Small letters of names and the words, "Love" and "Mommy"

Noticing my staring, one boy gave me a piece of carrot
Nibbling it quietly my ears sting when he said, "My mommy
makes too much food for me!"
"Ma...food?"
"Does your mommy make food?"

When I think of food, it's always fast food.
"Do you want pizza?"
Nod.
"How about KFC?"
Nods...
"I'm getting us McDonald's tonight."

~+~

For the first time, these eyes of mine are stinging but not from
the light

boiling up hot wetness against my vision
that's when I realized she never did so
never had i felt so gone

So I'm always left wondering...
Wandering
Hungering for a warm meal
By her hand.

Not Fully Burnt Out *Jocelyn Mulgado*

All I have to do is look at her
by Subhaga Crystal Bacon

my mother bragged, proud of her parenting, the perfected *look*.
    The look that said *don't you dare. Don't even think about it.*
What are you, stupid? The look that froze from across a room.
    In third grade I went to school half days. Sometimes morning
sessions that finished at lunchtime, when I did finish and didn't sit
    in the ketchup and milk carton smell of the cafeteria
daydreaming instead of working. Or when I did finish with the others,
    walking home in that sharp Kodachrome light, to watch
General Hospital. Those days she worked at the laundromat, cleaning
    the washers, removing lint from dryers. She needed to work, my mother—
and who can fault her—even riding the bus one town over to wipe
    the machines and look over the laundry. She needed to get out.
Afternoon sessions, my father would come sometimes to rescue me
    from the cafeteria, my work either done or not done.
My father in his dungarees and boots and Carhartt jacket, a laborer
    who didn't want his wife to work. She used to tell us in her dreamy way
what her life would be if she had never married, been a *professional woman*
    with her little laundry hand-washed and her apartment where she
lived alone. We could see her there. Instead, she perfected *the look*.
    The one she gave without seeing.

when the stars fall like lures
by Carella Keil

ocean waves caress the sun
the moon glides across the sky
like a lover's tongue

fishing for dreams
in the moonskin river
a smile like yours
comes along once
every 10,000 years

I bury my heart in the sand for safekeeping

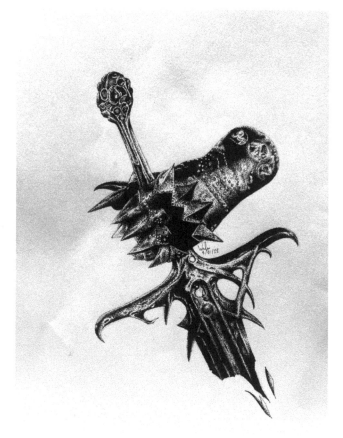

Untitled *Weather Castro*

Chilaquiles
by Wendy L. Silva

We are riding the night's lower back
　　　　like western women, hair wet
　　　　　　　　with Idaho spring and the breath of red
　　　　wine, when she rolls her tongue
on the cold back

　　　　of the spoon and says ice cream
tastes better like this.

　　　　I tell her *she* tasted better
　　　　　　　　like this
　　　　before going to my knees right there,
in the kitchen. She lets my mouth take her
　　　　　　　　in waves—smoky

onion and salt water scent, the flavors
　　　　of earth and lemon
　　　　　　　　rinds. She wants to move

　　　　　　　to the desert, wants to start a revolution,
　　　　　　　　　and all I can think about is
　　　　　　　　　　her hands

　　　　dicing tomatoes, ripping
　　　　　　　tortillas to fry with eggs
on Sunday mornings.

We'll always have chilaquiles, she says, and falls
　　　　asleep rubbing my nail between her fingers
　　　　　　　the way she did her mother's
　　　　　　on long car rides,

　　　　　　　reading each groove like a memoir
　　　　in braille. Perhaps, as her mind is taken
　　　　　　　　by the winds of sleep, she is still
trying to find her mother's life

　　　　in my hands,
　　　　　　　because I am a woman and isn't that enough
　　　　to make us feel a little closer
　　　　　to what we've lost?

Convict Chronicles: The Rapping at the Door
by Leo Cardez

Join me as we attempt to navigate a prison known as simply as Savageville. Savageville is a massive concrete and iron human warehouse surrounded by razor wire topped forty-foot walls. As you enter, notice the despair and fear floating in the sad dead eyes of row after row of caged young black men.

Cell: A grey, concrete, right angled rectangle with no outlets. Cellmate (aka Celly): Kin-Kin, short, chiseled, and hard with a shaved head and an air of the streets that can be neither taught nor faked.

Now you are among them as a recently convicted felon unready to serve a sentence of no less than 25 years—most will never breathe free air again. As a middle-aged, middle-class, educated white man you don't yet comprehend the gang-controlled hierarchy or convict code of the concrete jungle. You have no real connection or similarities to the majority of your fellow convicts beyond being of the same human race.

Fast forward a month. You know every inch of your tomb, every scratch of your steel door. You have paced your 4 feet of walkable space like a tiger in the zoo…just like the thousands before you. You have suffered indignities perpetrated by the very people tasked with your protection. You have fought against the mind games of the apex predators seeking easy prey. You have choked down 3 insipid meals a day shoved through a hole in your cell door like an animal during the "feeds". You have endured freezing 5 minute showers in rust-stained, mold-infested, cages once a week. You have anxiously talked with the few remaining loved ones who've stood by your side throughout this ordeal on your allotted 10 minutes a week—they have so many questions, you have so few answers. As night comes you begin to realize you are falling deeper into the well with every passing day—the light becoming dimmer. You ponder the easy way out. The coward's solution, you know, but even a rock will turn to dust with enough pressure.

Cut to Day 107. It's hours after "lights out". You lay on your bunk in the darkness and hear someone rapping a deep lyrical rhythm. Have you finally unmoored? Are you floating off into the abyss? You squint as you search for the source. It is your celly. He is sitting on the floor next to your iron door looking out through the sliver of a window. "You don't mind if I spit some beats?" he asks. You're happy for the distraction. You listen to his stories of the drug game, the hustle, the pain and the dreams. You begin to see yourself on the wings of his narrative sages. You realize everyone has shed blood, be it in different mud. Eventually you let your anxiety ridden exhaustion overtake you and slip off.

The "count lights" flicker on, the clickety clack of the food cart returns, you open your eyes only to realize the music has stopped and your nightmares are no match for your reality.

~+~

Prison is a fever dream of the upside down world of Stranger Things, but it has a lot to teach us as well. To survive in the shadows on the fringes of society you have to learn a new code for living; you have to learn to humble yourself while still fighting the stigmas trying to label you as subhuman; you even have to learn a whole new language.

In many ways, I was intrigued; especially by my celly's late night rap sessions. It took me days, and Kin-Kin's help, to decipher the lyrics (Do you know what "getting small" and "cutting off someone's water" means?) and weeks to truly understand their deeper meaning. Prison raps are their version of current history and a reflection of their truths. It is how they carry and pass along their culture. It was my first real awareness of how different cultures can coexist so closely and yet be worlds apart.

We all grow up with music and rap is mainstream now, but do we ever think about its historical and cultural importance? Do we consider its ability to bridge gaps or about how it connects us? In many ways inmates are dead but not yet buried, spending whole lifetimes in America's array of grey crossbar hotels, yet these raps are passed from generation of inmates to another. They are carried with as much care as any precious memory we hold dear. These are more than just music. They are the soul, prayers, and history of a marginalized people struggling to be heard.

Can you hear them? Will you?

Slowing Down
by David James

"I can sum up everything I've learned about life in three words: it goes on." - Robert Frost

Five inches of new snow in the driveway calls out to me and I hear my tractor, with its lawnmower still attached, swearing in the garage. "Get the hell out here," it yells, "and put on the frigging plow." My snow shovels tremble against the wall, trying to blend in with the rakes.

Of course, there's the drip in the kitchen faucet: "Over here. Over here. Over here. Over here." And I need to go Christmas shopping, do the laundry, empty the dishwasher, make sure to add those three English courses to the winter schedule. The phone rings. Coffee's done. I have eleven emails. My guitar gives me that *come hither* look. I need to read. I should work out. I have presents to wrap.

As I take out a pork loin for dinner, the five inches of snow laughs and plays in the wind. I'm stuck. Stuck in the window looking out as my life gets buried in the too-much-here and the more-than-I-need-now. All I can do is stare at the bright world, clean and cold, while my feet sink in quick-drying cement.

I can't move, dammit, but everything around me does.

Car Boyz
By Paul Lamar

In the rearview mirror at the light: two young
men in a Honda SUV. Driver: white, red-haired, bushy
beard, granny sunglasses, tapping the wheel to some
music. Passenger: South Asian, black wavy hair in a wide
white headband, granny sunglasses, clutching a big cup of
something from Five Guys, a straw poking through the lid,
which he toys with and sips from, looking down, mostly, but
sometimes stealing a glance at the driver, shy, smiling, scared,
giddy, in love. With the driver.
We move.
I call them Steve and Mike. Steve, the driver,
calls Mike Mikey, and Mike likes that. They are freshman
hallmates.
Steve is from Shushan, NY, in Washington County.
He likes tubing on the river just across the dirt road from his
house. Mike is from Hempstead, Long Island, but here he is
at college in Oneonta, a small city. If his mother knew he was
riding in a car driven by a boy his own age who had brought
the car from home against the college rules and stored it in
a garage in town, to say nothing of holding hands with this
boy, an inconceivable idea, of course---well, she would say,
eyes glistening, that his father was turning over…"you know
where, Zehen."
It is November.
Already Mike is thinking about auditing an
environmental science course that Steve is taking next
semester even though Mike is a business major, to become a
CPA. Maybe.
But he's not going back to Hempstead. The world
seems bigger than Long Island, even in a nowhere place like
Oneonta.
Is this love? He has never said it to himself. It wasn't
really sex either. It was on a mid-September college get-to-
know-you hayride. Steve was talking to twins from Syracuse,
Anna and Carl; but he was, under the straw, holding Mike's
left hand with his right.
Electrifying.
Steve has never spoken about it, and neither has
Mike, but they hang out every day.
Their car pulls even with ours in the left lane.
Mike looks over and sees me and Bill and nods, nods at two
70-year-old husbands in a 2014 Chevy Impala, the gift to

us by my 93-year-old blind father. We are on our way to the nursing home.

At the red light, now side by side, I give him a thumbs up, and he half-smiles again, uncertain why a bald man with a grey goatee is giving him a sign. He sips and moves his head to some beat that Steve is tapping out.

Off the line first, the SUV slips in front of us and takes the next right towards the Southside Mall.

DONORS

DELPHIC ORACLE
Jo Scott-Coe

EPIC BARD
Anonymous

PATRON
Gillian S. Friedman, MD
Dr. Tammy Kearn
Dr Kathleen Sell

MENTOR
Dr. Thatcher Carter

GUILD MEMBER
Anita Alfonso
Andre Davis
Yolanda Harrison
Wendy Silva

CONTRIBUTOR NOTES

Mikey Bachman (she/her, they/them) is an Associate Faculty member in the English Department at RCC and MVC. She received her MFA in Creative Writing, Poetry from Cal State Long Beach in 2019. When she isn't reading, writing, or planning classes, she spends her free time playing lots of PC games, and hanging out with her wife, Caro, and her Bichon Frise, Coco.

Subhaga Crystal Bacon (she/her) is a Queer poet living in rural Washington on unceded Methow land. She is the author of four collections of poetry including *Surrender of Water in Hidden Places*, *Red Flag Poetry*, and *Transitory*, forthcoming in the fall of 2023 from BOA Editions.

Growing up, **Briseyda Batz** would paint on the walls, not knowing the consequences. She did this up until she got caught painting on what was once her Tia's closet. Rather than get in trouble, however, her Tia went on to tell her mom about it and bragged that Briseyda could one day make something with this talent. Briseyda is now 18 and has been drawing since she could hold a pencil in her hand. She hopes that one day, her art will be recognized in wide regions.

Photographer **Jacob Bowling** shoots "Fleeting Clew" in San Francisco. Jacob is an aspiring professional still using his Nikon d3100 from high school and puts his art in the edit. His Instagram @jacobsbowling captures moments of his life through his eyes.

Leo Cardez is an award-winning inmate, memoirist and playwright. This is his first piece to appear in this publication. He can be reached at Leo.Cardez.Writer@gmail.com.

Weather Castro is a traditional artist with a love of fantasy and the macabre. Her works are often inspired by her equal love of cinema, television, and games such as Dungeons and Dragons. She would describe her works to be experimental as she appreciates the use of many methods. Though her favored techniques are stippling which allows her to imbue her works with gloominess, and acrylic painting.

James Coats is a poet, performer, and educator born in Los Angeles and raised in the Inland Empire. He believes that poetry has the ability to bring diverse groups together, offering a way to connect through shared challenges, achievements and experiences. He is the winner of the 2021 San Gabriel Poetry Slam. You can find him attending poetry readings throughout California or follow his poetry via his Instagram @MrLovingWords.

Brian Daldorph teaches at the University of Kansas. His most recent publications are *Kansas Poems* (Meadowlark P, 2021) and *Words Is a Powerful Thing: Twenty Years of Teaching Creative Writing at Douglas County Jail* (U Kansas P, 2021).

Dale Dewey is a New Jersey resident that has a new lease on life after trusting Jesus for his salvation. He likes to draw and works as a road laborer.

M. A. Dubbs is an award-winning Mexican-American and LGBT+ writer who hails from Indiana. For more than a decade her writing has been published in literary magazines and anthologies across the globe. In 2022 she released her first chapbook, *An American Mujer*, with Bottlecap Press. She was also nominated for a Pushcart Prize from *Oyster River Pages* and served as a judge for Indiana's state Poetry Out Loud competition.

Leah Felty is an artist from Moreno Valley, CA, who is currently pursuing her B.F.A in Animation/Illustration at CSU Long Beach. Her goal is to become a Character Designer and Visual Development Artist for animation, while running a small business selling her original artwork.

Sometimes on weekend mornings **Christopher Goldsmith** will go for a long bike ride or watch soccer on the Spanish television station. His work has appeared in *Sky Island Journal, Drunk Monkeys*, and last year he was nominated for a Pushcart. His wife Kelly occasionally mentions that the poem isn't right.

Ivana Gonzalez is a 21-year-old college graduate with dreams of making it big in the writing industry. For now, though, she's just working on transferring to a university where she will work toward a Master's Degree in English. A recent graduate of Riverside City College, Ivana isn't new to the writing gig. A former MUSE editor herself, Ivana is excited for the opportunity to see her own work inside the magazine she once helped create.

Claudine Grigg's fiction has appeared in *Lightspeed, Escape Pod, Zahir Tales, New Theory, Leading Edge SF, Not a Pipe Publishing, Upper Rubber Boot Books, Mount Island, Ligeia, Flora Fiction*, etc. Her story "Helping Hand" appears as an episode in the Netflix series "Love, Death & Robots." Her first novel, *Don't Ask, Don't Tell*, was released on

June 1, 2020, and a book-length story collection, *Firestorm*, was released on March 13, 2022. She has two nonfiction books out regarding trans/gender issues as well. Claudine is a long-time member of the Authors Guild and a member of Science Fiction Writers of America.

Born and raised on the third coast, Michigan, **David James** has published numerous books, chapbooks and one-act plays. After 45 years of working in higher education, James retired in 2022 in order to devote himself to "living."

Jeni (she/they) is a Xicana artist and RCC/UCR alumnus from the Inland Empire who identifies with the Rasquachismo artistic movement. As such, they are a working-class artist who utilizes various forms of traditional and nontraditional mediums. Their "water bear x plant" series expresses land-based spirituality and evokes sentiments of interconnectedness, resistance, resilience, and adaptability in the face of increasing social isolation fueled by our settler-colonial condition.

Zeima Kassahun is an Ethiopian-American visual artist originally from MUHFUKKIN RIVERSIDE. She is an Arborist living in Oakland, CA, and working for Friends of the Urban Forest, a non-profit based in San Francisco. Her art ranges from canvas to ceramics and is a visual representation of the things she often forgets. She enjoys drinking tea, being alone in nature, and adoring her kitties.

"If my writing leaves you feeling emotionally transparent, or sad, or aroused, or inspired to create castles out of seashells and bits of broken dream, then I know I've done my job as a writer, and have touched your soul." **Carella Keil** is a writer and digital artist in Canada. instagram.com/catalogue. of.dreams twitter.com/catalogofdream

Paul Lamar lives with his husband, Mark, in Albany, NY, where he teaches, reviews theater for a local paper, and conducts a chorus. His poems and stories have been published in Muse (2014), As It Ought to Be, Sand Hills Magazine, San Pedro River Review, etc.

Jordan Loveland is a graduate student in their last year of an English program in Creative Writing. They are a writer of the strange but meaningful and they enjoy dark humor and speculative fiction. A librarian and a nerd, Jordan is never without a book, daydream, or current obsession. They are a disabled, queer author who is a curator of the weird.

Joyce Meyers taught English for a number of years, then practiced law in Philadelphia for nearly three decades, focusing on litigation in defense of the First Amendment. Her poems have appeared in The Comstock Review, Atlanta Review, Iodine Poetry Journal, Caesura, Slant, and Evening Street Review, among others. In 2014 she won the Atlanta Review International Poetry Competition, and was nominated for a Pushcart Prize the same year. Her collections include *The Way Back* (Kelsay Books 2017) and two chapbooks, *Shapes of Love* (Finishing Line Press, 2010) and *Wild Mushrooms* (Plan B Press, 2007).

Kendal McGinnis is a writer and stand-up comic from Southern California and currently a Master's student in the Program for Writers at the University of Illinois Chicago. Her work has appeared in Cipher, Leviathan, and elsewhere, and she's been a runners-up for the Saints and Sinners Short Fiction Contest.

Alexandra Geiger Morgan is a psychotherapist who integrates the expressive arts into her treatment approach. Her work has appeared in Persimmon Tree, The RavensPerch, The Closed Eye Open, The Artisan, Down in the Dirt, The Woven Tale Press, among others. She lives in sunny St Petersburg, FL.

Alondra Montes Martinez is a Mexican American artist born and raised in Riverside, CA. She was first introduced to art by her family and from then on, her love grew. She first started off with painting landscapes with acrylic paint. As she continued, she discovered other forms of artistic mediums that don't only involve painting. She found a love for reading, writing, poetry and. She wishes to continue her artistic journey to lend her voice and creativity to her community.

Jocelyn Mulgado is an artist from Upland, CA, who specializes in surrealism, realism, and portraiture. Her style and artwork derives from her beliefs in mental health awareness, feminism, Chicano culture, and Christianity. With the fascination of nature and the human figure, Jocelyn creates whimsical pieces ranging in mediums from acrylic paint, oil paint, pen, and color pencil. Jocelyn Mulgado is currently studying at Azusa Pacific University, majoring in the arts with a concentration in drawing and painting.

Katherine Muñiz is a mixed media artist. She focuses on using various mediums to create an innovative body of work. She pulls from different tools such as her artistic skills, industrial ingenuity, and incorporating fiber and metal to her art to shape her ideas and concepts. Threading various materials allows her work to shift perspectives and evoke emotion. This unique style highlights her individuality as she challenges and breaks the boundaries of traditional art.

Zach Murphy is a Hawaii-born writer with a background in cinema. His stories appear in Reed Magazine, Still Point Arts Quarterly, The Coachella Review, Maudlin House, Eastern Iowa Review, and Flash: The International Short-Short Story Magazine. He lives with his wonderful wife, Kelly, in St. Paul, Minnesota.

Oyeleye Mahmoodah is the author of *Faded Blues*, the winning novel for the Nigeria Prize for Teen Authors 2021 and The Campus Journalism Awards, 2022. She is a member of the Hilltop Creative Arts Foundation. The link to her works published in literary journals is at linkfly.to/mahmoodahoyeleye . She tweets @Oye_Mahmoodah.

Joseph Perez is a street photographer residing in downtown Riverside, CA. He has a bachelor's in English Literature from California State University, San Bernardino. After taking courses in photography while earning his bachelor's, his passion for documenting life with a camera began.

A much-published bi-national immigrant, gardener, Bonsai-grower, painter, **Jennifer Phillips** grew up in upstate N.Y. and has lived in New England, London, New Mexico, St.Louis, Rhode Island, & now Cape Cod, Massachusetts. Her chapbooks: *Sitting Safe In the Theatre of Electricity* (i-blurb.com, 2020) and *A Song of Ascents* (Orchard Street Press, 2022).

Cati Porter's latest poetry collections are *small mammals* (Mayapple Press, 2023), *The Body at a Loss* (CavanKerry Press, 2019) and *Novel* (Bamboo Dart Press, 2022). Her poems have most recently been published in One Art, Terrain, Verse Daily, and Rattle. Find her at www.catiporter.com.

Beth Brown Preston is a poet and novelist with two collections of poetry from the Broadside Lotus Press and two chapbooks of poetry. She is a graduate of Bryn Mawr College and the MFA Writing Program at Goddard College. Her work has been supported by the Hudson Valley Writers Center and the Sarah Lawrence College Writing Institute. She has been published in numerous literary and scholarly journals.

Welcome to the punk side! The creator of **Artistic Punk** is Kennia pronounced (Ken-knee-uh). She has been doing art for about 5 years, she is also a certified graphic designer, and has her own art apparel line. Doing art has helped her express her emotions that she wasn't comfortable expressing yet. In hope, she wants to help others practice expressing their emotions as well as she did.

Imari Rede is a queer, latina poet from Riverside, CA. She loves sharing images and ideas that make people feel something. She's an RCC alumna who had her first published poem printed in RCC MUSE in 2017 titled "Desktop Cactus." Since then, she has published works of poetry in small publications such as Orange Mercury and Young Ignorantes. Her most recent live readings have been a mixture of poetry and comedy.

J.B. Rossi is a California native currently residing in the South Bay.

Théa-Marie Ryde was recalled to life amidst a global pandemic. When not writing or rearing her son, she works at Riverside City College, using her Buddhist practices to heal her newfound queer shanga. "Dispatches from the Wilderness" is her twenty-fifth published work — yet the first under her true name.

Claire Scott is an award winning poet who has received multiple Pushcart Prize nominations. Her work has appeared in the Atlanta Review, Bellevue Literary Review, New Ohio Review, Enizagam and The Healing Muse among others. Claire is the author of *Waiting to be Called* and *Until I Couldn't*.

Wendy L. Silva is a queer, Latinx poet from Santa Maria, CA and the proud daughter of Mexican immigrants. She did her undergraduate studies in creative writing at UC Riverside and received her MFA in poetry from the University of Idaho. She currently teaches English, Latinx literature, and creative writing at Riverside City College.

J. Tarwood now lives in China, and has five books: *The Cats in Zanzibar, Grand Detour, And For The Mouth A Flower, What The Waking See, The Sublime Way,* and the forthcoming *The World At Hand.* He has always been an unlikely man in unlikely places.

Victor Valencia is a Native American artist that works as a crane operator in CA. His hobbies consist of cooking, and being with his family. His Native American heritage inspires him to reveal his art authentically. He often references his art from ancestral Native American history to tell the unspoken truth for those who no longer can or whose voices have been silenced. Every detail reveals the depth of the moment in a specific way and the use of watercolor brings the bleak past to the reality of the moment.

Laura D. Weeks is a recovering academic who moved West and moved on. Originally a Slavist with a PhD from Stanford University, she has turned editor, translator and founder of a piano studio. Her translations, both scholarly and literary, have appeared widely, as have her poems. She is the author of two chapbooks, *The Mad Woman* and *Deaf Man Talking*.

Cherie Woods is a two-time Emmy award-winning producer turned educator working with high school students. She is a mother of four, three humans, and one miniature Goldendoodle. She remains an avid artist working in acrylic and felt mediums, currently residing in San Diego, CA with her family.

Madi Zins (she/her) is from Catonsville, MD, but she currently lives in New Orleans. Madi is interested in intersectional, ecofeminist poetics and tries to create poetry with images and themes of nature that are multifaceted and often contradictory. Her work has been published in Quail Bell Magazine, Antigravity Magazine, and mx.communication. Madi studied English Literature and Environmental Studies at Washington College. Her biggest poetic influences are Lucille Clifton, Joy Harjo, and Ross Gay.

Holden Vaughn Spangler Award

Submit up to 3 poems about a child or childhood
Winner receives $200 honorarium and publication
in the Spring 2024 edition of RCC *MUSE*

Email submissions to muse@rcc.edu
mail or hand deliver to:
Holden Vaughn Spangler Memorial Award
RCC *MUSE* Literary Journal
James Ducat, Editorial Advisor - Quad 21A
Riverside City College
4800 Magnolia Avenue, Riverside, CA 92506

Please send as an email attachment in .doc or .docx or .rtf format with
"Last Name – Genre – Title of Submission" in the subject line
(e.g., Smith – Prose – "In Summer").
Please do not put submissions in the body of the email.
$5 submission fee, payable to RCC MUSE by check or cash;
Venmo @RCCMUSE
No submission fee for RCC students with current id

MUSE is based in the Inland Empire in California, a place of rich diversity, and we are especially looking to publish work from underrepresented or misrepresented groups, such as people of color, disabled people, LGBTQ+, present and formerly incarcerated people, and others from a culturally and linguistically diverse background. We seek and welcome writers of all races, sexual orientations, gender identities/expressions, disability, religions, classes, veteran status, and educational backgrounds.

SUBMISSIONS OPEN 9/15 - 12/15
·All submissions must be typed.
·Include separate cover sheet with your name and all contact information, including email, phone number, address, and a short (approx. 75 word), third-person bio.
·We accept simultaneous submissions. Let us know if the work is accepted elsewhere.
·Authors and artists receive one copy of the issue in which their work appears. Contributors may also purchase additional copies.
·MUSE acquires First North American Serial Rights to the work you submit and non-exclusive reprint rights (for use in promotion, etc.).
·Should the piece be published elsewhere in the future, we ask that you acknowledge MUSE as first place of publication.
·Do not send revisions unless our editors have requested them.

We appreciate your patience; we try to respond to
all submissions within six months.

RCC MUSE · General Submissions

MUSE is based in the Inland Empire in California, a place of rich diversity, and we are especially looking to publish work from underrepresented or misrepresented groups, such as people of color, disabled people, LGBTQ+, present and formerly incarcerated people, and others from a culturally and linguistically diverse background. We seek and welcome writers of all races, sexual orientations, gender identities/expressions, disability, religions, classes, veteran status, and educational backgrounds.

Genres:

Prose - submit one short story or creative nonfiction piece
(up to 1500 words max)
Poetry - submit up to three poems

Email submissions to muse@rcc.edu
mail or hand deliver to:

RCC *MUSE* Literary Journal
James Ducat, Editorial Advisor - Quad 21A
Riverside City College
4800 Magnolia Ave, Riverside, CA 92506

Please send as an email attachment in .doc, .docx, or .rtf format with "Last Name – Genre – Title of Submission" in the subject line (e.g., Smith – Prose – "In Summer"). Please do not put submissions in the body of the email.

SUBMISSIONS OPEN 9/15 · 12/15

· All submissions must be typed.
· Include separate cover sheet with your name and all contact information, including email, phone number, address, and a short (approx. 75 word), third-person bio.
· We accept simultaneous submissions. Let us know if the work is accepted elsewhere.
· Authors and artists receive one copy of the issue in which their work appears. Contributors may also purchase additional copies.
· MUSE acquires First North American Serial Rights to the work you submit and non-exclusive reprint rights (for use in promotion, etc.).
· Should the piece be published elsewhere in the future, we ask that you acknowledge MUSE as first place of publication.
· Do not send revisions unless our editors have requested them.

*We appreciate your patience; we try to respond to
all submissions within six months.*

MUSE

RCC *MUSE* 2023 was designed using the following:

TITLE FONT - Menken Std Head Narrow

INTERIOR FONT - Adobe Jenson Pro

ALTERNATE FONT - Gotham

TRIM SIZE - 5″x 8″

INTERIOR - color printed on 70 lb. white paper

PERFECT BOUND - matte color laminated 80 lb. duplex cover

CPSIA information can be obtained
at www.ICGtesting.com
Printed in the USA
JSHW071531250523
42217JS00007B/27

9 780996 041195